JULIANE'S STORY...

A **real-life** account of her journey from Zimbabwe

Created by
Andy Glynne
Illustrated & designed by
Karl Hammond

In memory of Katy Jones, without whom this project would have never been possible.

This paperback edition published in 2016 by Wayland
First published in hardback in 2014
Text and Illustrations © Mosaic Films 2014

Wayland, Carmelite House, 50 Victoria Embankment, London NW1 3BH

Mosaic Films, Shacklewell Lane, London E8 2EZ

Created by Andy Glynne
Illustrated and designed by Karl Hammond

Editor: Debbie Foy
Layout design: Sophie Wilkins

Dewey ref: 362.7'7914'092-dc23

ISBN 978 0 7502 9282 5
eBook ISBN 978 0 7502 9347 1
Lib eBook ISBN 978 0 7502 7894 2

Printed in China

10 9 8 7 6 5 4 3 2 1

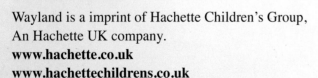
Wayland is a imprint of Hachette Children's Group,
An Hachette UK company.
www.hachette.co.uk
www.hachettechildrens.co.uk

JULIANE'S STORY...

My name is Juliane.
This is the story of my journey
from Zimbabwe.

WAYLAND
www.waylandbooks.co.uk

My mum and I lived on a farm when I was very young.

When I was three and a half my mum left me. I don't know why she left, but I think people were trying to kill her.

People from the church took me in and brought me up.
I had to learn to be my own mother and my own father.

I began to think that I had no parents.

But deep down I knew that my mum
was out there, somewhere,
looking for me.

In the orphanage there would be
around 30 children trying to
eat from one plate.

It was a really big plate, but there was only a tiny amount of food on it. It was only enough to feed one child.

I didn't eat much.
The only thing
I survived on
was water but it
wasn't clean.

The water was full of snails
and other dirty stuff, but
you had no choice –
you had to drink it.

The other kids in the
orphanage could be quite
mean. They'd laugh
at you and call
you names.

While the other kids were playing, I'd sit there on my own,
reading my book or just crying and watching the others play.

One day they
took us from the
orphanage and
loaded us into
a big, dark lorry
with hundreds of
other people.

Because I was the little one, I got on last,
so I was close to the back door.

All of a sudden I saw a lady. She had no shoes on.
All she was wearing was jogging bottoms and
a T-shirt. She was running after
the lorry and screaming
my name!

I looked at her and thought, 'I remember that face'. It was my mum! I started crying and trying to get out of the lorry.

I know it sounds really strange now, and I don't know how or where I got the power to do it, but I jumped from the back of the lorry straight onto her.

We were holding each other, screaming and crying. I couldn't believe it was real. From that point on everything turned around in my life...

My mum went to the authorities and eventually they gave me a visa to travel.

Not long after, we boarded a plane and arrived in our new home country.

I was happy to be back with my mum, but my first day at school was quite tough.

I mumbled a lot because
I was too afraid to
speak to people.

I often became anxious and had panic attacks. Sometimes when I sat in class I had no idea what was going on. It scared me.

In the back of my mind, I had the awful thought that perhaps my mum would not be there when I got home!

At times like these, my heart would beat really fast and sometimes I would even pass out.

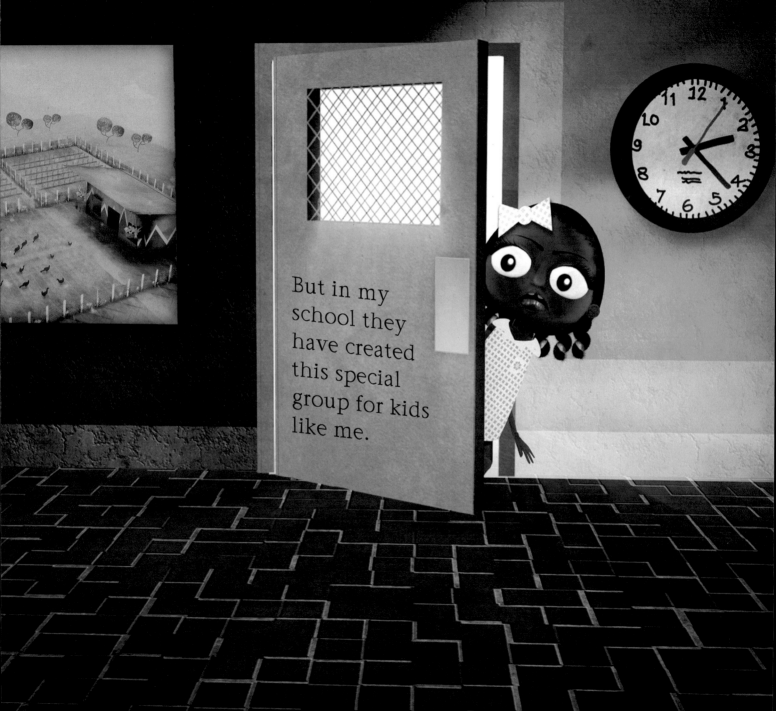

But in my school they have created this special group for kids like me.

Whenever I'm feeling angry, sad or anxious, I go there and there is always someone I can talk to. They try to help me and fix things as much as possible.

I'm really improving my social skills now, because I know that I'm a fighter and I'm a survivor.

I've learnt that no matter how much you go through and no matter how much you suffer, one day you'll be accepted for who you are.

One day you're going to be a shining star.

And I know that
at the end of every dark
tunnel in your life, there's
always a rainbow...